MW01601363

Un Pagan

Christianity

Exploring the Real Roots of Our Church Practices

Brad Chase

Contents

Preface

The book is meant as a follow up to those who have already read the book *Pagan Christianity* by Frank Viola and George Barna.

It was written to bring to light the biblical roots to Christianity that were omitted in Pagan Christianity and to help give another perspective on the Institutional church.

Although the content shared in this book challenges Frank and George's perspective (The Authors of Pagan Christianity), what unites us (our love for Christ) is far greater than what divides us.

I hope you enjoy another look at the *Un* Pagan Roots of the Institutional Church.

Introduction: What Really Happened to the Institutional Church?

666 is the sign of the devil and the devil wants to divide the church so he can conquer it. You see the devil at work in John 6:66:

> As a result of this, many [of] his disciples returned to their former way of life and no longer accompanied him.

Even the closest followers of Jesus became divided.

We read that "many of his disciples returned to their former way of life". These disciples didn't like what they heard from Jesus so they left him and his 12 apostles. The 12 apostles had deeper roots than the other followers and they chose not to leave him.

What caused the division?

The Eucharist.

The Eucharist is THE issue that still divides Christians today and one that the Institutional Church still places at the center of worship as Christ taught on the night of the Last Supper.

And this was just the beginning. We are warned of what is to come:

2 Timothy 4:3-4 - For the time is coming when people will not endure sound teaching, but having itching ears they will accumulate for themselves teachers to suit their own passions, and will turn away from listening to the truth and wander off into myths.

Men like St Basil, St John of the Cross, and many others have been fighting these divisions since the very beginning. Here is a look at some of those divisions:

- The Apostles were divided over the issue of whether or not Gentiles should be circumcised to become Christians and as a result, the first church council was held in AD 50 to resolve the issue: The Council of Jerusalem, Acts 15.

More divisions took place in the first 4 centuries as false teaching and false doctrine arose:

- Gnosticism (Not to be confused with Agnosticism) stated that God created the heavens and a lesser divinity created the material universe.
- Marcionism was a heresy that claimed the God of the Old Testament was a God full of wrath that was different from the loving God of the New Testament.
- Docetism was the heresy that stated Jesus was not truly human.
- Arianism was a heresy which holds that Jesus Christ is the Son of God, who was begotten by God the Father, and is distinct from the Father (therefore subordinate to him), but the Son is also God the Son but not co-eternal with God the Father.

Heretics would often attempt to prove their position from scripture.

Many times they didn't even want huge changes. For example, the Arians wanted to add one letter (the Greek letter yoda) to the word homoousion which would change the meaning from "one in being" to "similar in being".[1]

---

[1] Ignatius of Antioch is the first person recorded using the words "Catholic Church" in 107 in his Letter to the Smyrnaeans. He speaks about Bishops in this letter as well:

In addition to all of these divisions above, it would have been impossible for first-century Christians to worship like we do today because Christianity was illegal.

At the end of the first century, the book of revelation was written. Which is an interesting point. In the work of Pagan Christianity, there is a hypothesis that we should try to mimic worship of the first century Christians, but it's important to point out that for most of the first century, we did not yet have a complete bible.

Ignatius of Antioch is the first person recorded using the words "Catholic Church" in 107 in his Letter to the Smyrnaeans. He speaks about Bishops in this letter as well:

> "Wherever the bishop shall appear, there let the multitude [of the people] also be; even as, wherever Jesus Christ is, there is the Catholic Church."

Not soon after Christianity was legalized, the Germanic Tribes started taking over the Western Roman Empire. Rome was sacked in 410 by Goths and again in 455 by Vandals (which is actually where we get the word Vandalism).

By 476 there was no emperor in the western empire. There was still an emperor in Constantinople who claimed to be the emperor of all of Rome. Some consider 476 the date of the fall of the Roman Empire.

We can split the invading Germanic tribes who came into the western Roman empire into two groups:

Group 1: came in as Christians but the wrong kind of Christians: Arians

- Ostrogoths ended up in Italy and visigoths in Spain.

- Burgundians ended up in the part of France which is now called Burgundy.
- The vandals who took North Africa.
- They all came in as heretics from the point of view of the church.
- They were a military problem and a religious problem.

Group 2: Another set of Germanic tribes came in as pagans.

- The Franks went to what is now France.
- The Angles went to modern-day England.
- The Saxons stayed in England and some moved to modern-day Germany.

Before the Germanic tribes took over the western Roman Empire there was law and order. If someone came and tried to steal from you, you could report it to the local authorities and it would be handled. When the Germanic tribes took over there was no structure like the Roman government previously had in place.

Let's imagine some things that might come up. There is a famine, a food shortage, who do you go to? The local bishop.

We have stories of bishops from 6th century Gaul (now France) providing care for whatever was needed in the community.

Bishops were taking over what used to be civil authority.

Pope Gregory the Great lived in Rome at a time when there was no emperor. A plague hit and he was the one providing care for many of the sick people. He also convinced Attila the Hun to turn around and not sack Rome.

With no civil authority available to help, people thought maybe if I get God on my side he can help. So people started going to monks and hermits for help.

When the church started to take over civic duties a lot of people started to give money to the church in the form of Gold, money, buildings, and land.

It was around this time that the Church Council of Tours came to the conclusion that tithing should be a church practice.

Society starts to move from a money economy to a barter economy. And what is worth a lot of money?

Land!

A very broad estimate by the Middle Ages 12-13th century is that some church institutions (whether a bishop or monastery or whatever) owned a third of all the land in Europe. This is an estimate and could be off by quite a bit. Either way, this reminds us of how wealthy the church was getting.

Bishops accumulated wealth and power. Then Germanic leaders (kings) become interested in that wealth. Kings start to try to influence who becomes bishops.

As the church gets wealthier, kings try to get more and more involved. The line between church and state starts to become blurred.

Once the church has that kind of power and wealth, it's hard to give up.

This becomes the drama of the chapter in the church's life and leads to many bishops leading separate lives from the people. People stopped relating to the bishops because they had so much wealth and couldn't feel the real problems of society over time. [2]

---

[2] Cook, William R. 2009. *The Catholic Church: A History.*

It's one of the main reasons why St Francis appears on the scene around the beginning of the 13th century with the commission from God to "Rebuild My Church".

That work began and was successful to a large degree as we still have Franciscan orders today and a Franciscan Pope in Pope Francis.

Theologians

St Thomas Aquinas (Dominican) and St Bonaventure (Franciscan theologian- Augustinian) emerged as two great theologians in the 13th century. Both borrowed from Aristotle but Aquinas more than Bonaventure. But they draw the line with Aristotle as well. Both died in 1274.

Their theology could be considered Pagan since it borrows from Aristotle, but the Church, and most Christians, generally accepted their theology as true despite this.

But the divisions did not stop there.

In the 12 century, we see the growth of two very large heretical movements that rejected the sacraments.

- Dualist heresy and the Cathar or Albigensian heresy.

Then a series of heretical movements kicked off the Protestant reformation starting with Jan Hus who was burned at the stake, an admittedly low point in the Catholic Church, and continuing in the Protestant Reformation with Martin Luther and John Calvin.

From the time of Jesus until today, Satan has been hard at work trying to divide the church that Christ established.

An example of division at work is the misuse of this statement: **I believe**

In their book, Pagan Christianity, Frank and George make this statement: **I believe** the first century church is the church in its purest form before it was tainted.

While it's important to believe, it's important to separate your beliefs from your opinions and look at what the faithful of the church have taught since the time of Christ and passed down to subsequent generations. We will review the Apostles creed which also starts with the words "**I believe**" and see how it compares to what the authors of Pagan Christianity believe.

We will also revisit important church practices and their biblical roots, much of which was omitted in Pagan Christianity.

This book will connect the dots between Jesus and his 12 apostles to the 1 billion+ people who attend his church every day, every hour, and in nearly every country of the world and will show you the biblical roots that have kept the church in place and growing among the faithful in every country of the world for 2000 years.

It is my hope that you discover the gifts that Christ gave up his life to give you in his church and in the sacraments.

Warning! If you are not a member of the institutional church, this book will shock you. Finding out that God has been knocking on the door and waiting with Spiritual gifts may cause a radical change in your church, social, and family life. If you are ready to discover a whole new life in Christ through the gifts he promised you through the 12 apostles, then continue reading.

Chapter 1: Have We Really Been Doing it by the Book?

The premise of Pagan Christianity is built on the **beliefs** of the authors. Here is a quote from their book:

> *"I believe the first century church is the church in its purest form before it was tainted." - Frank Viola and George Barna* [3]

The facts presented in Pagan Christianity are then built on this belief while omitting other relevant facts that show the full picture of the church, even in the first century setting.

While the Pharisees and Sauducees were heavily criticized by Jesus for their religious practices, Jesus never condemned the Institutional Church of his time.

The growth of Christanity was NOT organic, it was intentional. It was not built by a movement of spirit filled home churches, although that definitely took place, rather it was built by a group of men who were given authority by Christ over the church and were sent out at Pentecost to build this church.

We find evidence of first century church organization in documents like the Didache, the Rule of Faith, and the Creed. We also find a catechetical school being formed by John the Apostle where these teachings continue.

---

[3] Viola, Frank, and George Barna. 2012. *Pagan Christianity*. N.p.: Pagan Christianity.

These were unified efforts by the Apostles and first century Christians to form the Institutional Church that is still here today.

Omission #1: Didache, 1st Century Document

The Didache, also known as The Lord's Teaching Through the Twelve Apostles to the Nations, is a brief anonymous early Christian treatise written in Koine Greek, dated by modern scholars to the first century. The first line of this treatise is "The teaching of the Lord to the Gentiles (or Nations) by the twelve apostles".

The text, parts of which constitute the oldest extant written catechism, has three main sections dealing with Christian ethics, rituals such as baptism and the eucharist, and church organization.

The opening chapters describe the virtuous Way of Life and the wicked Way of Death. The Lord's Prayer is included in full. Baptism is by immersion, or by affusion if immersion is not practical. Fasting is ordered for Wednesdays and Fridays. Two primitive Eucharistic prayers are given. [4]

Church organization was at an early stage of development. Itinerant apostles and prophets are important, serving as "chief priests" and possibly celebrating the Eucharist.

Meanwhile, local bishops and deacons also have authority and seem to be taking the place of the itinerant ministry.

---

[4] Liddell, Henry George; Scott, Robert (1940). "διδαχή". *A Greek–English Lexicon*. Revised and augmented throughout by Sir Henry Stuart Jones, with the assistance of Roderick McKenzie. Oxford: Clarendon Press. Cross, edited by F.L. (2005). *The Oxford dictionary of the Christian Church* (3rd rev. ed.). Oxford: Oxford University Press. p. 482. ISBN 978-0192802903. Retrieved 8 March 2016. "Didache." Cross, F. L., ed. *The Oxford Dictionary of the Christian Church*. New York: Oxford University Press. 2005

Omission #2: The Rule of Faith

Prior to the council of Nicea, each church had their own rule of faith (though all were very similar), which contained the central tenets of Christianity memorized at baptism by all new Christians.

The Rule of Faith was referred to as "The Rule" and "The Rule of Truth".

Clement of Rome (*written anonymous from the Church at Rome*), A.D. 95-96

Let us give up purposeless and fruitless cares and approach **the holy and venerable rule of our calling**. Let us attend to what is good, pleasing, and acceptable in the sight of him who formed us. Let us look steadfastly to the blood of Christ and see how precious that blood is to God, which has set the grace of repentance before the whole world. Let us turn to every age that has passed and learn that … the Lord has granted a place of repentance to all that would be converted to him. Noah preached repentance, and as many as listened to him were saved (First Clement 7).

Irenaeus, A.D. 183 - 186

The one who retains **the rule of the truth** received through baptism unchangeable in his heart will surely recognize the names, the expressions, and the parables taken from the Scriptures [by the gnostics] but will by no means acknowledge the blasphemous use which these men make of them (Against Heresies I:9:4).

Omission #3: The Creed

A creed is a statement of faith with the goal of preventing confusion and heresy among believers. It was the most primitive way to say, this is what our faith is all about.

There is evidence of a creed in Judaism called the Shema Yisrael.

The Shema has been described as a confession of faith. Whenever the people of Israel renewed their covenant with God they reminded themselves of these terms (Deuteronomy 30:19).

Renewal of the Covenant usually took the form of a vow or oath.

Declarations of the covenant renewal were typically stated aloud. The verb typically used to denote this action was "confess" or "confess with your lips".

Greek speaking Jews used the word "homologia" for their statement of faith. Christians continued this practice with the formation of the creed.

Traditional twelve articles of the Creed

The Catechism of the Catholic Church presents the creed in the traditional division into twelve articles:

1. I believe in God the Father almighty, creator of heaven and earth.
2. I believe in Jesus Christ, his only Son, our Lord.
3. He was conceived by the power of the Holy Spirit and born of the Virgin Mary.
4. Under Pontius Pilate, He was crucified, died, and was buried.
5. He descended to the dead. On the third day he rose again.
6. He ascended into heaven and is seated at the right hand of the Father.
7. He will come again to judge the living and the dead.
8. I believe in the Holy Spirit,
9. the holy Catholic Church, the communion of saints,
10. the forgiveness of sins,
11. the resurrection of the body,
12. and the life everlasting.

The Err of the Pharisees and Sadducees

In their book *Pagan Christianity*, Frank and George describe how the unbiblical traditions of the Pharisees and Sadducees added and subtracted from Holy Scripture to leave us with something that is far from what God intended.

Were the Apostles also guilty of this err when writing the Didache, using the rule of faith, and forming the Apostles Creed?

This book will explore the biblical roots of the church practices that are considered Pagan by Frank and George in their book *Pagan Christianity*.

When Jesus died and rose from the dead, he gave birth to his church. That church was himself in another form.

But right before he died, he made a peculiar statement in John 19:30: **It is Finished.**

We will dive deeper into the meaning of this statement in subsequent chapters.

Chapter 2: The Church Building

Did early Christians have priests, sacrifices, and buildings?

It's easy to answer one part of that question: No, they did not have buildings called churches. And why would they, Christianity was illegal and Christians were being killed for their faith.

The authors of Pagan Christianity claimed that Jesus ended the Ancient practices of Judaism which included the priesthood, sacrifices, and church buildings. Since Jesus is the high priest and the perfect sacrifice, the work is complete and needs no addition or subtraction. Consequently the temple, the priesthood, and the sacrifice all passed away with the coming of Jesus Christ.

But in the days before the Temple, God was carried in an Ark, and before the Ark God had no physical dwelling place on Earth. The Ark and the Temple were given to the people over time, just as God gave Christians their churches over time.

So where do church buildings really come from? Pagan sources? And what about priests and sacrifices, did Jesus really end the priesthood when he came as the high priest and allowed himself to be offered as a sacrifice?

To understand the answers to these questions, let's go back and look at how the priesthood developed and what it foreshadowed.

The First Priest

The first mention of a priest in the bible is a mysterious figure Melchizedek in Genesis 14:18. He kind of just shows up on the scene and then isn't heard of again (with the exception of a quick mention in Ps 110:4) until Jesus mentions him.

Jesus invokes Melchizedek as a symbol of a new spiritual priesthood (hebrews 7:15–19) where Jesus does not exercise a priesthood through family lineage but through his immortal existence (Hebrews 7:15–16), fulfilling Ps 110:4 (Heb 7:17; cf. Heb 7:3).

Thus he abolishes forever both the levitical priesthood and the law it serves, because neither could effectively sanctify people (Heb 7:18) by leading them into direct communication with God (Heb 7:19).

Does that mean no more priesthood?

Lets dive a little deeper.

The Work of the Apostles

When Jesus recruited the 12 Apostles to follow him, he left them with a mission and the mission had some specific instructions:

1. Matthew 28:19-20 - Go, therefore, and make disciples of all nations, baptizing them in the name of the Father, and of the Son, and of the holy Spirit, teaching them to observe all that I have commanded you.

2. Luke 22:19 - Then he took the bread, said the blessing, broke it, and gave it to them, saying, "This is my body, which will be given for you; do this in memory of me.

3. John 20:21-23 - [Jesus] said to them again, "Peace be with you. As the Father has sent me, so I send you." And when he had said this, he breathed on them and said to them, "Receive the holy Spirit. Whose sins you forgive are forgiven them, and whose sins you retain are retained."

It's apparent that Jesus gave his 12 apostles a mission: To baptize, to eat his body and blood, and to forgive sins. In this chapter we are going to take a deeper dive into what happened to this mission and how it relates to the church.

Church Buildings, Sacred Objects, Relics, and more

Frank and George make a laundry list of Pagan practices that were introduced to the church such as:

- Sacred objects
- The sign of the cross
- Relic mongering
- Using altars for false sacrifices
- Using candles
- Burning incense
- Being spectators at mass
- Pagan temples
- Sacrifices
- Altars
- Passive laity
- Preaching
- Sunday worship
- East facing temples
- The building itself and more

Let's consider one thing: Were these practices the central part of worship?

The Glaring Omission from Pagan Christinaity: No!

This is not what was important to first century Christians. Jesus didn't die because the Sabbath was on the wrong day, or because someone said a sermon and lit a candle in an unauthorized building that smelled like incense.

Jesus died for our sins and gave us ways to receive grace through the Sacraments at the hands of the priests. All of the additional points argued here are secondary. What has always been important in the Institutional church are:

- **Sacraments**
-
- **People with Authority to administer those sacraments**

The Church has existed with all of the extras mentioned above and without them as well. No where in the book *Pagan Christianity* do the Authors make a legitimate statement about what is fundamental to 1st century Christians, the sacraments: Baptism, Confirmation, The Eucharist, and the Forgiveness of Sins.

Lets go back to the Pagan practices that Frank and George mention in their book *Pagan Christianity* to see if there are any biblical roots to these practices:

- Biblical sources for the sign of the cross:
    - Genesis 4:15 and Exodus 12:7 depict marks that were used for saving purposes.

    - The prophet Ezekiel saw the righteous in Jerusalem would one day be saved because of a mark upon their foreheads.

      What was that mark?

      According to the ancient rabbis it was Taw, the last letter of the Hebrew alphabet, which in ancient times was drawn as a cross.

- Biblical sources for sacred objects
    - Some objects are so sacred that God struck down people for mistreating them. When Uzzah touched

the sacred ark of God, he was struck dead 2 Samuel 6:6-7.

- Biblical sources for relic mongering
    - 2 Kings 13:20–21: Elisha died and was buried. Now Moabite raiders used to enter the country every spring. Once while some Israelites were burying a man, suddenly they saw a band of raiders; so they threw the man's body into Elisha's tomb. When the body touched Elisha's bones, the man came to life and stood up on his feet.

    - Acts 19:11–12, which says that Paul's handkerchiefs were imbued by God with healing power.

    - The bleeding woman that was healed after touching Jesus garment: Mark 5:25-34.

    - Those who touched the tassel on Jesus cloak were healed: Mark 6:56.

    - Also cited is the veneration of Polycarp's relics recorded in the Martyrdom of Polycarp (written 150–160 AD).

- Biblical sources for the altars
    - Altars were used to sacrifice animals in the old testament to the true God, not Pagan Gods. After Jesus was circumcised, two doves were offered for sacrifice. Luke 2:24. Altars were erected by Abraham (Genesis 12:7; 13:4; 22:9), by Isaac (Genesis 26:25), by Jacob (33:20; 35:1–3), and by Moses (Exodus 17:15).

- Biblical sources for candles

- Lampstands were used for ritual celebration in the old testament: Numbers 8:1-4 and Exodus 25:31-40.

- Biblical sources for holy water
    - Numbers 5:17, Leviticus 15, 16, and 17:15.

- Biblical sources for burning incense
    - Exodus 30:1; 30:7, 37:25; 40:5, 26, 27, 2 Chronicles 13:11, 1 Chronicles 28:18, 2 Chronicles 2:4, Leviticus 16:12-13.

- Biblical sources for temples
- Solomon built a temple: 1 Kings 6.
- Biblical sources for passive laity
    - This does not sound passive: Didn't Paul address this exact question 2000 years ago? 1 Corinthians 10:16 - The cup of blessing that we bless, is it not a participation in the blood of Christ? The bread that we break, is it not a participation in the body of Christ? Our participation is not identified by singing and speaking in tongues, it's defined by taking his body and blood (the Eucharist), according to Paul, which the Institutional church has been doing since the Last Supper.

- Preaching
    - Explained in detail in the Chapter 4 of this book.

- Biblical sources for east facing temples
    - Ezekiel 47:1 - Then he brought me back to the entrance of the temple, and there! I saw water flowing out from under the threshold of the temple toward the east, for the **front of the temple faced east.**

- Biblical sources sunday worship

- Exodus 20:8-11, Mark 2:27, Leviticus 23:3, Genesis 2:3, Isaiah 58:13, Hebrews 4:9.

- In addition, for the Romans everyday was a pagan day of worship. Sunday was to honor the sun god. Monday was to honor the moon god, and so on until Saturday or Saturn-day. Sunday worship comes from the tradition of keeping the Sabbath holy.

The church building is born out of the love and generosity of the people who desire to give God a dwelling place, much like King Solomon.

Jesus himself took part in pilgrimages and in festivals. He prayed spontaneously and formally, kneeling, standing, and prostrate. He worshipped alone, with congregations, and with friends. He recited the Scriptures. He went on silent retreats away from the bustle and distraction of the world. It is our privilege to imitate him in this beautiful variety. And our tradition gives many ways of doing so.

But none of this replaced the Passover for Jesus. As a faithful Jew, Jesus never skipped the Passover to worship in a different way. He still subscribed to the religious practices of the day despite his criticism of some of the practices and attitudes of these religious leaders.

Not all prayers and devotions are created equal. There is something more important than singing, praying in tongues, and fellowship..

Jesus gave the 12 apostles **four** primary tasks and we see these tasks continuing after their death:

1. **Baptism**: We see baptism being carried out in Acts 2:41, Acts 16:15, Acts 16:30, Acts 2:38-39. The apostles passed down this authority to baptize. Phillip baptized in Acts 8:12 and Acts 8:35-40.

2. **Eucharist**: The Lords supper, otherwise known as the Eucharist, was well established after the apostles. Writing around the middle of the second century, Justin Martyr gives the oldest descriptions of something that can be recognised as the rite that is in use today, according to K.W. Noakes. Earlier sources, the Didache, The Epistle of Clement, and Ignatius of Antioch provide glimpses of what Christians were doing in their eucharists. Later sources, Tertullian and the Apostolic Tradition (an early Christian treatise), offer some details of the Eucharist from around the year 200. Once the Church "went public" after the conversion of Constantine the Great in the second decade of the fourth century, it was clear that the Eucharist was established as a central part of Christian life.

3. **Confession**: John 20:19-23: On the evening of that first day of the week, when the doors were locked, where the disciples were, for fear of the Jews, Jesus came and stood in their midst and said to them, "Peace be with you." When he had said this, he showed them his hands and his side. The disciples rejoiced when they saw the Lord. [Jesus] said to them again, "Peace be with you. As the Father has sent me, so I send you." And when he had said this, he breathed on them and said to them, "Receive the holy Spirit. Whose sins you forgive are forgiven them, and whose sins you retain are retained." James 5:14-16: Is anyone among you sick? He should summon the presbyters of the church, and they should pray over him and anoint [him] with oil in the name of the Lord, and the prayer of faith will save the sick person, and the Lord will raise him up. If he has committed any sins, he will be forgiven. Therefore, confess your sins to one another and pray for one another, that you may be healed. The fervent prayer of a righteous person is very powerful.

4. **Preaching**: Matthew 28:19-20 Go, therefore, and make disciples of all nations, baptizing them in the name of the

Father, and of the Son, and of the Holy Spirit, <u>teaching</u> them to observe all that I have commanded you. And behold, I am with you always, until the end of the age."

Did baptism, the Eucharist, and Confession end with the 12 Apostles? Or did that work carry on?

Ignatius of Antioch, who had been a disciple of the apostle John and who wrote a letter to the Smyrnaeans about A.D. 110, said: Wherever the bishop appears, there let the people be; as wherever Jesus Christ is, there is the Catholic Church. It is not lawful to baptize or give communion without the consent of the bishop. On the other hand, whatever has his approval is pleasing to God. Thus, whatever is done will be safe and valid.

— *Letter to the Smyrnaeans* 8, J.R. Willis translation.

Justin Martyr, wrote, "Not as common bread or common drink do we receive these; but since Jesus Christ our Savior was made incarnate by the word of God and had both flesh and blood for our salvation, so too, as we have been taught, the food which has been made into the **Eucharist** by the Eucharistic prayer set down by him, and by the change of which our blood and flesh is nourished, . . . is both the flesh and the blood of that incarnated Jesus" (First Apology 66:1–20).

Origen, in a homily written about A.D. 244, attested to belief in the Real Presence of Christ in the **Eucharist**. "You are accustomed to take part in the divine mysteries, so you know how, when you have received the Body of the Lord, you reverently exercise every care lest a particle of it fall and lest anything of the consecrated gift perish" (Homilies on Exodus 13:3).

St. Cyprian: "The apostle [Paul] likewise bears witness and says: ' . . . Whoever eats the bread or drinks the cup of the Lord unworthily will be guilty of the body and blood of the Lord' [1 Cor. 11:27]. But [the impenitent] spurn and despise all these warnings; before their sins are expiated, before they have made a **confession of their crime**, before their conscience has been purged in the ceremony and at the hand of the priest . . . they do violence to [the Lord's] body and blood, and with their hands and mouth they sin against the Lord more than when they denied him" (The Lapsed 15:1–3 (A.D. 251]).

Origen "[A final method of forgiveness], albeit hard and laborious [is] the remission of sins through penance, when the sinner . . . does not shrink from **declaring his sin to a priest** of the Lord and from seeking medicine, after the manner of him who say, 'I said, "To the Lord I will accuse myself of my iniquity"'" (Homilies on Leviticus 2:4 [A.D. 248]).

Who carried out these sacred tasks?

The successors of the Apostles and their co-workers: the priests and deacons (more on preaching in Chapter 4).

As in the previous Covenants of the Old Testament, sacred tasks are eventually carried out in a church building. We see this trend continuing in Christianity.

Chapter 3: The Order of Worship

In their book Pagan Christianity, Frank and George mention some things which, in their opinion, are the reasons the institutional church "got it wrong":

- In the institutional church, everyone is passive and muted in the Liturgy.
- You will never find anything that remotely resembles something like our order of worship.
- Roman Catholic mass has few points of contact with the New Testament.
- Authors say that the headship of Christ should run Christian meetings and the meetings should resemble new testament worship: Every member functioning, spontaneity, vibrancy, and open participation as outlined in 1 Corinthians 14:18.

We might not have heard the specific words "Go to Church" until Clement of Alexandrea spoke those words in the 2nd century, but Jesus did make reference something very peculiar a number of times:

1. Jesus makes reference to "the hour".
2. Jesus said "It is finished" when it seemed as though it wasn't quite finished (more on this in Chapter 9).

The answers to these two questions will clue us in to what and how Jesus intended us to worship and how early Christians actually worshipped.

The Hour

There are four times in the bible where Jesus makes a statement that seems out of place regarding "**the hour**".

1. The wedding at Cana, John 2: On the third day there was a wedding in Cana in Galilee, and the mother of Jesus was

there. Jesus and his disciples were also invited to the wedding. When the wine ran short, the mother of Jesus said to him, "They have no wine." [And] Jesus said to her, "Woman, how does your concern affect me? **My hour has not yet come**."

2. Samaritan woman at the well. John 4:21: Jesus said to her, "Believe me, woman, **the hour is coming** when you will worship the Father neither on this mountain nor in Jerusalem.
   a. John 4:23: But **the hour is coming**, and is now here, when true worshipers will worship the Father in Spirit and truth.

3. John 5:25: Amen, amen, I say to you, **the hour is coming** and is now here when the dead will hear the voice of the Son of God, and those who hear will live.

4. John 12:20-24- Now there were some Greeks among those who had come up to worship at the feast. They came to Philip, who was from Bethsaida in Galilee, and asked him, "Sir, we would like to see Jesus." Philip went and told Andrew; then Andrew and Philip went and told Jesus. Jesus answered them, "**The hour has come** for the Son of Man to be glorified. Amen, amen, I say to you, unless a grain of wheat falls to the ground and dies, it remains just a grain of wheat; but if it dies, it produces much fruit."

   And what does a grain of wheat produce when it dies? Bread.

Why would Jesus say "The Hour" has not come? It doesn't really make sense, unless he is referring to the future when the hour will occur. And when it does happen what is Jesus going to do?

In the hour:

- He is going to provide provisions of wine.

- He is going to provide a new way of worship that includes everyone (Jews and Gentiles) and they will worship in Spirit and Truth (**preaching**).
- He is going to have a whole new way to hear the word of God (**from the bible, specifically the New Testament**) which will help us pass from death to life.
- And last but definitely not least, in "the hour" he will be providing provisions of bread (**the Eucharist**), because we know that a grain of wheat must die to produce bread as Jesus died to become that bread for us.

And where do we see all of these things occurring? During the hour of the Mass that the Institutional church has practiced continually since its inception at the last supper.[5]

St Justin martyr liturgy checklist

St Justin Martyr describes the liturgy of his time in the 2nd century. It is almost identical to the liturgy of the Institutional Catholic Church today, nearly two millennium later:

From the First Apology of St. Justin Martyr, c. 155 AD

> *" No one may share the Eucharist with us unless he believes that what we teach is true, unless he is washed in the regenerating waters of baptism for the remission of his sins, and unless he lives in accordance with the principles given us by Christ.*
>
> *We do not consume the eucharistic bread and wine as if it were ordinary*

---

[5] https://youtu.be/m3Db1lXdufg

food and drink, for we have been taught that as Jesus Christ our Savior became a man of flesh and blood by the power of the Word of God, so also the food that our flesh and blood assimilates for its nourishment becomes the flesh and blood of the incarnate Jesus by the power of his own words contained in the prayer of thanksgiving.

The apostles, in their recollections, which are called gospels, handed down to us what Jesus commanded them to do. They tell us that he took bread, gave thanks and said: Do this in memory of me. This is my body. In the same way he took the cup, he gave thanks and said: This is my blood. The Lord gave this command to them alone. Ever since then we have constantly reminded one another of these things. The rich among us help the poor and we are always united. For all that we receive we praise the Creator of the universe through his Son Jesus Christ and through the Holy Spirit.

On Sunday we have a common assembly of all our members, whether they live in the city or the outlying districts. The recollections of the apostles or the writings of the prophets are read, as long as there is time. When the reader has finished, the president of the assembly speaks to us; he urges everyone to imitate the examples of virtue we have heard in the readings. Then we all stand up together and pray.

On the conclusion of our prayer, bread and wine and water are brought forward. The president offers prayers and gives thanks to the best of his ability, and the people give assent by saying, "Amen". The eucharist is distributed, everyone present communicates, and the deacons take it to those who are absent.

The wealthy, if they wish, may make a contribution, and they themselves decide the amount. The collection is placed in the custody of the president, who uses it to help the orphans and widows and all who for any reason are in distress, whether because they are sick, in prison, or away from home. In a word, he takes care of all who are in need.

We hold our common assembly on Sunday because it is the first day of the week, the day on which God put darkness and chaos to flight and created the world, and because on that same day our savior Jesus Christ rose from the dead. For he was crucified on Friday and on Sunday he appeared to his apostles and disciples and taught them the things that we have passed on for your consideration."

As Justin described, the Eucharist today is still restricted to baptized members of the institutional church, the church still teaches that the Eucharist is more than just bread, we still assemble on Sundays as they did then, the bible is read during the liturgy and then we pray, communion is brought forward, prayers of thanksgiving are offered, the people still say "Amen", the Eucharist is still distributed, and a collection is taken up.

The Liturgy of the Mass of the Institutional church has been preserved in nearly every way that Justin Martyr outlined in the 2nd century.

Lets compare what we learned to the "ideal meeting" described in Pagan Christianity (this meeting is based on 1 cor 12):

- 30 people came
- Someone started a song
- Everyone joined in
- Prayers between the songs
- Songs sung several time
- Then we sat down
- Woman stood up and shared what the lord did for her
- Others stood up to share with what the lord said
- Someone sang another song.
- Someone shared a poem
- Everyone shared what they had experienced with the lord that week.
- None of this was planned.
- It was electric
- Jesus was leading the meeting. (Matthew 18:20 where two or more are gathered in my name, I am there with them - so this is true).

This is an amazing description of the Holy Spirit at work. There is a movement in the Institutional Church Called "Life in the Spirit" and this is exactly what the meetings look like.

HOWEVER!

As mentioned above "The hour" is not just referencing worship in spirit and truth, there are three other elements that Jesus alluded to that need to be present.

The order of Worship today in the institutional church is nearly identical to the order of Worship among the first Christians.

Chapter 4: The Sermon

Ferdinand was born in 1195 in Portugal. He grew to be a pious kid. Don Martin, his father, was disappointed when Ferdinan decided to become a priest. It's not the path he had envisioned for his son.

At the age of fifteen, Ferdinand joined the Canons Regular of <u>St. Augustine</u> in Lisbon.   Two years later, he transferred to the monastery in Coimbra to avoid the distractions from frequent visits of relatives and friends.   During this time, he studied diligently, and being gifted with an excellent memory, he attained an excellent knowledge of theology, Sacred Scripture, and the Church Fathers.

Meanwhile, the Saracens (Arab Muslims) had been killing Christians and were becoming a larger threat to the people of Portugal.

The Saracens were eventually defeated on July 16, 1212 at the Battle of Las Navas de Tolosa. Ferdinand was convinced that his fervent prayers to defeat the Saracens helped secure the victory.

Ferdinand became a priest.

He continued to pray that the cruel Saracens would never enter Portugal again. He came to the realization that if people were to go and preach the faith in North Africa, they could convert their enemy and save their souls. On January 16th 1220, 5 Franciscan missionaries had been cruelly murdered for doing the exact thing Ferdinan had been praying about: Preaching in North Africa.

The bodies of these men were sent back to Coimbra where Ferdianan lived and that experience changed the course of his life. He heard a strong voice in his heart saying: You too are going to Africa.

To pursue this desire, he left the Augustinians and joined the Order of Friars Minor, the Franciscans, and took the name "**Anthony**."

Ferdinan decided that he could live the life of a saint if he courageously went to North Africa to continue preaching the Gospel like the men who had just given their lives for the faith. He joined the Franciscans.

He left for North Africa to preach but on the way he became very ill. He never preached a word in North Africa and was taken back to Portugal. On his way back to Portugal a hurricane was approaching and caused the ship to change course and took them to Sicily.

While in Sicily, it became known to Anthony and his companions that Francis was holding an assembly with all the Friars. Anthony wanted to meet Francis so they made the trip to the assembly. Anthony was still not well so the trip took much longer than expected and Anthony did not arrive until the final day when all of the assignments were handed out.

Not knowing what to do with Anthony, Francis asked Anthony to go live with a group of Friars that had limited access to a priest (Franciscans were not priests in those days). This way the Friars could receive the sacraments and since there were no other available assignments left by the time Anthony had arrived, he had no other choice.

He became the cook of the new house. He found joy in serving his 3 brothers in his new home.

Another group of Religious called the Friars Preachers (Dominicans) had a joint event one day with the Franciscans . When everyone arrived at the event, the Dominicans assumed that the Franciscans would provide someone to give a sermon at the event since they were the hosts of the event and the Franciscans assumed that since the Domincans order was preaching, that they would be providing someone to give a sermon.

Embarrassed, the Franciscans scrambled to find someone. Anthony, with no preparation, was asked to speak on behalf of the Franciscans since he was a priest.

Anthony gave a powerful homily that shocked both the Franciscans and the Dominicans. The Franciscans asked, isn't this the man who was doing the dishes for a few of our brothers. The Domincans asked, who is this Franciscan who speaks so eloquently.

After this event St Francis realized that Franciscans could live simple lives and still be highly educated.

Are Sermons Pagan

This is a great story, but only a great story if it's true that priests SHOULD be giving sermons. Is this a Pagan practice or is there any historical evidence that Sermons were being given prior to the time of Constantine?

In their book *Pagan Christianity*, Frank and George show the Pagan roots to sermons. However, there is clear evidence that Jesus preached:

> He gave the Sermon on the mount in Matthew Chapters 5-7. Peter also preached to a large crowd after Pentecost and converted nearly 3000 people from that speech (Acts 2:14-40). Stephen preached in Acts 7:1b–53.

Jesus personally gave his Apostles four primary tasks: Baptize, Forgive sins, Feed his Sheep (Eucharist), and to teach, one way to teach is is to preach:

- Matthew 28:19-20 Go, therefore, and make disciples of all nations, <u>baptizing</u> them in the name of the Father, and of the Son, and of the holy Spirit, <u>teaching</u> them to observe all that I have commanded you. And behold, I am with you always, until the end of the age."

St. Justin Martyr

And on the day called Sunday, all who live in cities or in the country gather together to one place, and the memoirs of the apostles or the writings of the prophets are read, as long as time permits; then, when the reader has ceased, the president verbally instructs, and exhorts to the imitation of these good things. Then we all rise together and pray, and, as we before said, when our prayer is ended, bread and wine and water are brought, and the president in like manner offers prayers and thanksgivings, according to his ability, and the people assent, saying Amen; and there is a distribution to each, and a participation of that over which thanks have been given, and to those who are absent a portion is sent by the deacons. (St. Justin Martyr, First Apology, chap. 67)

In the "First Apology" of Justin Martyr (c. lxvii) we read: "On the day called Sunday, all assembled in the same place, where the memorials [apomnemoneumata] of the Apostles and Prophets were read . . . and when the reader has finished, **the bishop delivers a sermon**", etc.

In this connexion, the "Encyclopaedia Britannica" (ninth edition) says: "The custom of delivering expositions or comments more or less extemporaneous on the lessons of the day at all events passed over soon and readily into the Christian Church" [i.e., from the Jewish synagogue].

From this the Catholic view differs, and maintains that the kind of homily referred to by Justin was not a continuation of the Jewish commentary on Scripture, but was an essential part of Christian worship, a continuation of the Apostolic sermon, in fulfilment of Christ's commission to His disciples. Both indeed had an external similarity (see Luke 4:16-20), but in essence one differed from the other as much as the Christian religion differed from the Jewish.

In their book Pagan Christianity, Frank and George claim that the sermon freezes the listeners and makes them inactive in the participation of the celebration.

This thinking ignores scripture when Jesus taught the masses who were undoubtedly frozen in their seats, it ignores Jesus' call to teach everything he has commanded the Apostles to do in Matthew 28.

Why preaching is important

Preaching is the call to teach in Matthew 28. Without teachers to guide the faithful, it would be hard to understand God's will through the scriptures and live that faith out.

This is apparent in Acts 8:26-31 when Phillip asks the Eunuch if he understands what he is reading:
> "Do you understand what you are reading?" He replied, "How can I, unless someone instructs me?" So he invited Philip to get in and sit with him.

Polycarp was a disciple of John the Apostle and many of the sermons that Polycarp gave have been preserved. This is evidence that sermons were a practice of the Apostles and early Christians.

Irenaeus (a Greek Bishop) states that on Polycarp's visit to Rome, his testimony converted many disciples of the heretical teachers Marcion and Valentinus.

Authors of Pagan Christianity Say Preaching is not Biblical

We see examples of preaching here:

- 1 corinthians 9:13-14 - Do you not know that those who perform the temple services eat [what] belongs to the temple, and those who minister at the altar share in the sacrificial offerings? In the same way, the Lord ordered that those who <u>preach the gospel</u> should live by the gospel.

- Jesus himself preached:
    - Jesus preached the sermon on the mount to 5000 people in Matthew Chapters 5, 6, and 7.
    - Jesus read a scripture passage and then gave an explanation, similar to a sermon. Luke 4:21: Jesus said "Today this scripture passage is fulfilled in your hearing."
    - Matthew 4:23, 9:35, and Luke 8:1 which says Jesus went out proclaiming the gospel.

- But probably the most convincing is Matthew 24:14 where Jesus says "And this gospel of the kingdom will be preached in all the world as a witness to all the nations, and then the end will come."

If Jesus did not want people to preach, why would he do it himself? Why would he say the gospel will be preached in all the world?

Chapter 5: The Pastor

A little boy named John grows up in France during the French revolution, a time when Christanity is being persecuted.

John is inspired by the heroic courage of the priests who risk their lives daily to celebrate the mass in secret.

The persecution of Christans ended and John began to study to become a priest. However, this was interrupted in 1809 when he was drafted into Napoleon's army.

He was drafted and was on his way to report for the war when he fell behind. If he did not report to his company by the end of the day he would be considered a deserter. The punishment for being a deserter was the death penalty and over 600 French soldiers had been executed during this time for deserting their company.

A man noticed that John was in distress and offered to help. They went deep into the mountains of Le Forez and John thought they were taking some sort of short cut to catch up to his company, but instead John was brought to the village of Les Noes, a hiding place for deserters.

A widow named Claudine Fayot took him in. During this time, French soldiers would often arrive unannounced searching for deserters. One day, John was caught off guard and could not get away in time and had to quickly hide.

He crawled underneath a haystack.

Hardly able to breath under the haystack he had to remain completely silent and still. A soldier walks by and draws his sword and starts to put his sword through the haystacks. John was stabbed by this soldier but was able to remain quiet and was able to remain hidden.

The wound was not fatal and John was able to recover.

An imperial proclamation in March 1810 granted amnesty to all deserters, enabling John Vianney to go back legally to Écully, where he resumed his studies.

He was not a great student and struggled to pass seminary.

It seemed he would never be able to become a priest due to his poor studies, however, Abbé Balley recommended that he be ordained due to his reverent prayer life. This request was approved and John Vianney became ordained and served as the assistant to Abbé Balley.

In 1818, shortly after the death of Balley, Vianney was appointed parish priest of the parish of Ars, a town of 230 inhabitants.

The town was not left with many faithful as a result of the French Revolution and its attack on The Church.

John Vianney began praying and fasting for his church community in Ars. He saw the people were spending their money and their time drinking and dancing. This was leading many souls in his community to sin.

He began preaching against drinking and dancing, urging people to stop this practice and sometimes refusing to absolve people of their sins in the confessional unless they vowed to give up this practice.

One time he took the money from the church and found the musicians that were going to be playing music at the bar later; he gave them their wage and asked them not to play that night.

He sought out the poor and the orphans. In 1824 he started La Providence, a home for orphan girls.

At one point he had so many orphans depending on him, he ran out of food and they were starving. He told the kids to gather together and pray for food because he knows the prayers of children are powerful with the Lord. After the prayer they found that the attic was miraculously full of grain, enough to feed them for an extended period of time.

The fight against drinking and dancing, his love for the poor and the orphans, his unfiltered preaching, his dedication to the confessional, and miraculous healings at his church gained him popularity in the surrounding communities.

By 1855 over 20,000 pilgrims a year were coming to Ars to visit this priest and his parish. He would spend 16-18 hours a day hearing confessions from all of the pilgrims visiting.

Where did the Pastor Come From?

In their Book *Pagan Christanity*, Frank and George claim the Pastor is not biblical.

Let's take a deeper look at that question by looking at the history of the priesthood.

A priest is an authorized mediator who offers sacrifice to God on behalf of others. Christ is the perfect priest, for he is perfectly united to God in his divinity and fully united to us in his humanity. Here is a good summary:

> Everything that the priesthood of the Old Covenant prefigured finds its fulfillment in Christ Jesus, the "one mediator between God and men" (1 Tim 2:5). The Christian tradition considers Melchizedek, "priest of God Most High,"

as a prefiguration of the priesthood of Christ, the unique "high priest after the order of Melchizedek" (Heb 5:10; Heb 6:20, Gen 14:18); "holy, blameless, unstained" (Heb 7:26), "by a single offering he has perfected for all time those who are sanctified" (Heb 10:14), that is, by the unique sacrifice of the cross.

Here is a breakdown of the priesthood in the Old and New Testament:

    I.   The Priesthood of the Old Testament
        A. The Patriarchal Period
        B. Israel, a Nation of Priests
        C. The Levitical Priesthood

    II.   The Priesthood of the New Testament
        A. The Priesthood of Christ
        B. The Common Priesthood of the Faithful
        C. The Ministerial Priesthood

I. The Priesthood in the Old Testament

A. The Patriarchal Period

The foundation for the religion of the patriarchs was the natural family order.

In this context, authority passed from father to son, and sacrifices were offered not at designated sites, but at the discretion of the patriarchs, who practiced a form of natural religion. Sacred actions included building altars (Gen 12:8), planting trees (Gen 21:33), offering sacrifice (Gen 8:20), and erecting pillars (Gen 28:11-22).

This action of sacrifice on altars was attributed to Pagan practices in the book Pagan Christinaity, but we can clearly see that the practices of the Institutional Church are in fact rooted in the early chapters of the Old Testament.

The origins of the priestly office, then, can be traced to the unique spiritual authority, representative function, and religious service of the father in the family.

At the same time, the office of kingship was the embodiment of the fathers secular duties, most notably his role in leadership and governing. The priesthood is inseparable from fatherhood (Job 1:5).

The archetype of the royal priesthood in the patriarchal period is Melchizdek, priest-king of Salem (i.e. Jerusalem, Ps 76:2). This mysterious figure is the first person in Scripture to be called a priest (Gen 14:17-20); he offers bread and wine to Abram (**Abraham**) and then gives his blessing to Abram and his men.

B. Israel, a Nation of Priests

The Old Testament traces the progress of sin and its terrible impact upon the human family-from Adam's fall to Israel's enslavement in Egypt, which is described in the beginning of Exodus.

We see a consistent pattern throughout the story: tragedy and sin lead to firstborn sons being disinherited (e.g. Cain, Ishmael, Esau, Reuben, Er, Perez, Manasseh).

The pattern in individuals would be repeated in Israel as a nation. Moses was told at the burning bush: "Israel is my firstborn son" (Exod 4:22). The importance of the firstborn is revealed in stark terms at Passover when Israel's firstborn sons are redeemed by the blood of the Paschal lamb. Thereafter, firstborn sons are consecrated to the Lord's service (Exod 13:2; 22:29).

"Go" commands Israel, his "firstborn son," to embrace its unique vocation and mission to be a "holy nation and a royal priesthood," to be a mediator between the Father and the family of nations.

That status, however, is entirely conditional (as the earlier examples of disinherited sons demonstrate) upon the adherence of Israel to the covenant: "if you obey my voice and keep my covenant you shall be my special possession" (Exod 19:5-6).

The Isrealites soon broke their fidelity to God by worshipping the golden calf, and the blessing of the firstborn was forfeited to the Levites when they avenged the Lord at the command of Moses (Exod 32:25-29). This event signaled the beginning of a second period of the priesthood in the Old Testament, the Levitical priesthood.

C. The Levitical Priesthood

As the book of Exodus reveals, Israel's apostasy with the golden calf at Sinai required a renewal of the covenant -- first with Moses alone (Exod 33-34), but then extended to Israel with the command to build a **Tabernacle** and consecrate **Aaron** as high priest (Exod 35-40).

God only then commanded Moses to speak to Israel about the types of sacrifice (burnt, sin, peace) that Aaron and his sons would be interested to offer on the people's behalf according to the priestly code (Lev 1-16).

Finally, the holiness code was given for the Levitical priests to instruct the twelve lay tribes of Israel (Lev 17-26).

The result was an elaborate system of priestly mediation based on the hierarchical order of Moses, Aaron (and his sons), the Levites, and the twelve tribes of Israel.

In the Old Testament, this same priestly hierarchy (high priest, Aaronic priests, and Levites) continued (with some minor variations) throughout the history of Israel: the wilderness period, the conquest and settlement of Canaan, the monarchy, and the period after the exile.

The result of Israel's second lapse into idolatry at Beth-peor (Num 25:1-13) was the imposition of the Deuteronomic covenant on the twelve tribes of the plains of Moab, the site of the new apostasy (Deut 3:29, 4:3).

When the Deuteronomic covenant was ratified, a two-covenant structure was instituted over the twelve tribes (Josh 8:30-35).

By its terms, Israel was placed under the administrative supervision of the Levites (Deut 27:9-26). The Levites for their part were bound by the "Covenant of Levi" (Jer 33:17-26; Mal 2:4-8), which was made with them by Moses at Sinai after the incident of the golden calf. The Levitical covenant was then renewed with the grandson of Aaron, Phinehas, at the end of Israel's forty years of wandering in the wilderness.

Phinehas was granted a "covenant of a perpetual priesthood" in recognition of his righteous zeal in avenging the second generation's idolatrous worship of Baal of Peor (Num 25:13).

In the time after the settlement of Canaan, the renewed covenant continued to exercise influence on the shape of the Old Testament priesthood, climaxing with the collapse of Eli's priestly house (1 Sam 2:27-36), the expulsion of Abiathar as high priest (1 Kgs 2:26-35), and the subsequent elevation of Zadok as high priest in Jerusalem (1 Kgs 2:35).

Crucial in this development was proving genealogical descent from Phinehas, something possessed by Zadok (1 Chr 6:4-8) but missing in Eli and Abiathar (1 Sam 22:9-20). The Zadokite high priesthood in the Jerusalem Temple became one of the distinctive features of the Davidic monarchy, at which time the Levites were given specialized ministries within the Temple (as Liturgical musicians, singers, guardsmen, treasurers, etc.; 1 Chr 9:22-34; 23:2-28).

The importance of Israel's high priests after the **Exile** is foreshadowed in Ezekiel's visions of the restoration of Jerusalem under the (Zadokite) high priest (Ezek 43-45). This situation is one means of explaining Zechariah's seemingly incongruous description of the royal crowning of the high priest **Joshua** (Zech 6:9-13), instead of **Zerubbabel**, the Davidic descendant who played a pivotal role in the rebuilding of the Temple (Ezra 5:2).

Further, this view is seen in the praise reserved by Sirach for the priestly figures from Aaron down to the high priest of his day, Simon, who is honored as "the leader of his brothers and the pride of his people" (Sir 50:1).

Sources outside the Bible further portray the Messiah as a combination of Davidic kingship and high priestly authority.

Messianic expectations and views of first-century A.D. Jewish Christians were seemingly influenced by this outlook, and the author of Hebrews makes it the basis of his argument concerning Christ's royal high priesthood "after the order of Melchizedek" (Heb 7).

The Zadokite high priesthood endured in Jerusalem until Antiochus IV Epiphanes (see Seleucids) deposed Onias II in 175 B.C. and replaced him with Jason (r. 175-172 B.C.). The Seleucid rulers then appointed non-Sadokites until they were defeated in 153 B.C. by the Hasmoneans, who continued the non-Zadokite rule until the Roman conquest in the first century B.C. The subsequent appointment of high priests was done only with the approval of the Herodian kings and the authority of Rome.

This custom lasted until the destruction of the Jerusalem temple in A.D. 70. With that event the last vestiges of the Levitical priesthood— and the Old Covenant—were extinguished.

II. The Priesthood in the New Testament

With the coming of Christ as God's firstborn Son (Heb 1:6), and royal High Priest (Heb 2:2-17; 5:1-10), the division of royal and priestly powers was brought to an end.

By establishing his Church as 'the assembly of the firstborn" (Heb 12:23), Christ reunited the offices of priesthood and kingship and restored the "royal priesthood" (1 Pet 2:9) of God's people, who now constituted the "Israel of God" (Gal 6:16).

The priesthood of Jesus must be seen in light of the Old Testament priesthood, and the full understanding of the New Testament priesthood should begin with the patriarchal period and the pace of the firstborn son. Luke 2:7 refers to Jesus as the "firstborn," which indicates that Jesus is entitled to receive all the rights and status of the firstborn under Mosaic Law (Exod 13:2, Deut 21:15-17).

It may be significant that, when Jesus was presented in the Temple (Luke 2:23), the redemption fee of five shekels (by which a Levite replaced a firstborn son in service to the Lord; Num 8:15-16) is not mentioned.

If so, it indicates that Jesus is consecrated to the service of the Lord instead of being "bought back" by his parents.

We would then see Jesus in the role of a priest by virtue of being a first son in the patriarchal sense.

A. The Priesthood of Christ

The Letter to the Hebrews gives us the fullest treatment of Christ's priesthood in the New Testament. According to its author, the priesthood of Jesus is defined in relation to the Levitical priesthood of Aaron, to which it is superior in every essential respect. Jesus is the sinless priest (Heb 4:15), whereas the Aaronic priests are sinners and must offer sacrifices for themselves as well as the people (Heb 5:1-3).

Jesus is the *everlasting* priest (Heb 7:24), whereas the Aaronic priests are mortal and must be replaced by an endless line of successors (Heb 7:23).

Jesus is the *heavenly* High Priest (Heb 4:14, 8:1-2), whereas the priests of the Old Covenant ministered in a sanctuary on earth (Heb 8:4-5). Jesus is the *royal* priest promised by oath in the Messianic Ps 110:4 (Heb 5:6; 7:17), whereas the Levitical priests took office without any oath at all (Heb 7:21).

As the more perfect priest, Christ offers the Father a more perfect sacrifice than any priests of the Levitical order could; Christ's sacrifice was offered once for all (Heb 10:10), in contrast to the continual cycle of sacrifices required under the Old Covenant (Heb 10:11). The reason is that Christ's sacrifice brought about a true remission of sins (Heb 9:11-14, 28; 10:12-18), in contrast to the Levitical offerings, which served as reminders of sin but were incapable of removing sins (Heb 10:4, 11).

The backdrop for these claims is the belief that Jesus belonged, not to the priestly order of Aaron, but to the patriarchal order of Melchizedek (He 5:6, 6:20).

This idea is developed in Heb 7, and is based on Psalm 110, which envisions the **Messiah** both as an enthroned King (Ps 110:1) and as a Melchizedekian priest (Ps 110:4). The idea is that Christ belongs to the original order of priesthood that was exercised in pre-Levitical times.

This explains why the author of Hebrews puts such stress on the sonship of Jesus in relation to his priesthood (Heb 2:10, 5:5-10). In particular, he emphasizes that Christ is the "firstborn" of the Father (Heb 1:6), who stands in relation to believers as both a brother (Heb

2:11-12) and a father figure (Heb 2:13-14). It is even possible that Melchizedek, who is both a forerunner and a **type** of Christ, was viewed in such terms by the author and original readers of Hebrews, who would have known that Jewish tradition identified Melchizedek with **Shem**, the firstborn son of Noah.

Other aspects of Melchizedek's priesthood point to Christ as well.

For instance, Melchizedek was the priest-king of Salem (Heb 7:1), which is an ancient name for Jerusalem or Zion (Ps 76:2). This priesthood-kingship of Melchizedek prefigures the royal priestly ministry of Jesus in the "heavenly Jerusalem" (Heb 12:22).

So, too, just as Melchizedek the priest brought for bread and wine (Gen 14:18), Christian reflection sees a prefigurement of the Eucharist, the sacrificial meal that Christ offers believers under the appearance of bread and wine (Matt 26:26-29).

B. The Common Priesthood of the Faithful

Christ, as High Priest and mediator, has made the Church "a kingdom, priests to his God and Father" (Rev 1:6). He has restored and fulfilled in himself the family priesthood of the firstborn, the vocation to which Israel was called, by sharing in the firstborn sonship and priesthood (cf. Exod 4:22, 19:6).

The people of God thus share in the dignity of Christ's priesthood through their baptismal participation in his mission as priest, prophet, and king, according to the individual vocations (1 Pet 2:5-9). By grace, the Church shares in the sonship of Christ, and thus shares also in his priestly mission.

The Church is entrusted with the vocation that had been intended for Israel among the nations.

C. The Ministerial Priesthood

The second participation of the faithful in the priesthood of Christ is through the ministerial or hierarchical priesthood. The two forms of participation are ordered one to the other, but they are essentially different (in kind and not simply in degree).

The common priesthood of the faithful is exercised through baptismal grace, whereas the ministerial priesthood serves and sanctifies the faithful and is passed on by the sacrament of holy orders.

Jesus chose the twelve apostles to serve as the heads of the new People of God (Matt 19:28; Rev 21:12-14).

As sharers in the one priesthood of Christ, itself of the order of Melchizedek, the apostles were to serve as the priestly firstborn sons, acting as elder brothers and fathers to the communities under their charge (cf. Acts 15:23, 1 Cor 4:15). In turn, the apostles appointed to succeed them elders or presbyters over the churches they had founded (Acts 14:23). Strictly speaking, the New Testament does not refer to Christian ministers as "priests" (Greek *hiereis*) but as "bishops" (Greek *episkopoi*) and "presbytrs" (Greek *presbyteroi*). Nevertheless, it is from this latter term that the English word "priest" is actually derived.

By virtue of the sacrament of holy orders, the priest acts in the person of Christ, the Head of the Church.

As Thomas Aquinas wrote, "Christ is the source of all priesthood: the priest of the old law was a figure of Christ, and the priest of the new law acts in the person of Christ". Ordained ministers make the presence of Christ as Head of the Church visible to the community. [6]

------

[6] Hahn, Scott. 2010. Many Are Called: Rediscovering the Glory of the Priesthood. N.p.: Crown Publishing Group.

Chapter 6: Sunday Morning Costumes

One day a homeless man walked into a church and the service had already started. He walked down the center aisle looking for a seat.

He smelled and wasn't wearing very nice clothes.

There was no place for him to sit.

The Pastor was in the middle of his homily.

As he went down the center aisle it was clear there was nowhere for him to sit down as the church was quite full that day. Nobody was about to scoot over to let him squeeze in either.

As he got to the front of the church you could feel the tension. People were uncomfortable.

What was this guy doing?

Instead of turning around he sat down on the ground in front of the first Pew. People were clearly distracted and the Pastor didn't quite know what to say. A man behind him stands up and approaches him to ask him to leave. Instead of asking him to leave, he sits down next to him and shakes his hand and welcomes him to the church.

The Pastor stops his sermon and speaks about the love of Christ between these two men and how a simple action of sitting down with someone and shaking their hand can be a powerful message and love and acceptance to those who are often shunned.

Dress Code

The institutional church has never imposed a dress code on its members. While the culture around the church changes and people like Horace bushnell (1843) affect the culture by starting a movement to dress up for church, the church itself has never imposed a dress code on its members.

The authors of Pagan Christanity were critical of the practice of wearing nice clothes to church claiming it is another manmade tradition but gave no Pagan root for this practice.

Clergy dress

The authors of Pagan Christianity argue that when a priest wears garments, it separates them from the other worshippers making two classes of people. They also claim that this dress code is Pagan since it was instituted by Constantine.

But they missed one critical question. Is the practice of priestly clothes (different from the clothes of other worshipers) from Pagan roots or rather from the roots of the old testament?

Exodus 28 describes the priestly vestments that Aaron and his sons (Nadab and Abihu, Eleazar and Ithamar) wore.

A priestly tunic (Hebrew ketonet), tunic: made of pure linen, covering the entire body from the neck to the feet, with sleeves reaching to the wrists. Those of the priests were plain (Exodus 28:40), while that of the High Priest was embroidered (Exodus 28:39).

If priestly vestments were part of the Old Testament, we can conclude that having a priest wear different clothes than that of the people is something God is ok with.

Pope Gregory I

One day, Pope Gregory saw some beautiful blonde slaves and asked who they were. He was told that those people are Angles (Germanic peoples who settled in Great Britain), he responded that they looked like angels and should be Christian.

So he sent monks to England to spread the faith. During this time he instructed the monks to keep parts of the culture to make them feel at home at church but not to lose the important things of the mass.

Incorporate the Culture

We can see that from a very early time from Constantine to Pope Gregory it has been important to keep parts of the culture to help people feel at home when they enter a church. This was seen in the time of Constantine and also in the time of Pope Gregory and throughout the centuries.

All of this is done with the intent to draw people in while keeping sacred things sacred, such as the Eucharist and the other sacraments.

Like the story given at the start of this chapter, everyone is welcome in the church.

Whether it is the richest of the richest in expensive clothing, or a poor homeless person sitting on the floor in the front of the church, the Institutional Church has never required a dress code to participate in the mass.

The only requirement to participate is Baptism and even then, people who are not baptized are still welcomed to sit and watch the Mass.

Perhaps Pope Gregory got this idea of keeping things from the culture from Pope Julius 1st. Romans used to celebrate the festival of Saturnalia to honor the God of Saturn from Dec 17th to Dec 23rd. Pope Julius 1st decided to celebrate the birth of Jesus on December 25th. This would absorb the Pagan Celebration of Saturnalia and turn the focus to things of Christ.

Chapter 7: Ministers of Music

The authors of Pagan Christianity claim that Jesus never sung a song, therefore we should consider choirs and singing unbiblical. The authors then go on to provide the Pagan roots of the Roman choirs.

Jesus may not have been in a choir, but he definitely sang songs, see Mark 14:26 and Matthew 26:30 where Jesus sung the Little Halel during the Passover liturgy.

In fact, music has always been part of the Passover meal.

In the celebration of Passover, Psalms 113-114 were recited during the Passover meal and at the conclusion of the meal the remaining Hallel Psalms (Psalms 115-118) were sung.

As a faithful Jew, Jesus would have participated in this musical liturgy every year at the Passover meal when the lambs were slaughtered and consumed to renew the covenant.

The Ideal Church Meeting

Frank (the author of Pagan Christianity) was in a meeting and it unfolded in what he describes as the ideal setting:

- 30 people came
- Someone started a song
- Everyone joined in
- Prayers between the songs
- Songs sung several time
- Then we sat down
- A Woman stood up and shared what the lord did for her

- Others stood up to share with what the lord said
- Someone sang another songSomeone shared a poem
- Everyone shared what they had experienced with the lord that week
- None of this was planned
- It was electricJesus was leading the meeting

This is a beautiful meeting filled with the Holy Spirit and enriches the lives of those who participate in it.

Music is part of the worship experience even for the authors of Pagan Christianity.

For Frank and George, the authors of Pagan Christianity, to conclude that singing is OK, but only in certain formats, is a bit of a stretch which is never confirmed in any way in the scriptures.

Chapter 8: Tithing and Clergy Salaries

They authors of Pagan Christianity point out that biblical tithing is not what we think it is.

Abraham did not give out of his need, he gave out of his abundance (Gen 14:20). The authors go on to say if we were to compare this to modern day scenarios it would be like winning the lottery and giving a tenth of the proceeds. Hardly generous. Abraham's tithe was voluntary, not compulsory.

The authors go on to say that giving 1/10 of our firstfruits actually isn't really something that is practiced in the bible. The Levites, for example, gave something more like 23.3% of their income, not just 10%. And the 23.3% was a product of the land, not necessarily income.

In Malachi Chapter 3:8-10 the tithes mentioned here are more like taxes. To the people of that time, a tithe was more like a tax that was required by law. So the condemnation of not tithing in Malachi would be similar to a condemnation of someone not paying taxes in a modern day situation.

If you look at all of these examples, we see no indication of a tithe to be imposed on any sort of regular basis, especially to pay for church buildings and pastors salaries.

But weren't there buildings in the Old Testament? And wasn't there a temple?

Even if we connected the temple tax paid in the Old Testament to show a sort of tax were to be paid, the Authors of Pagan Christianity go on to say that the unbiblical clergy system has been abolished and the old priesthood was crucified with Christ.

The authors go on to say Cyprian of Carthage was the first to argue that clergy should be supported by the tithe. Cyprian argues that since the Levites were supported by the tithe, the Christian clergy was to be supported by the tithe as well.

The authors of Pagan Christinaity come to this conclusion: **This is misguided thinking because today the Levitical system has been abolished.**

We can pause there to consider one question:

- If the system has **not been abolished but rather fulfilled**, it's quite possible that tithing is biblical as it was in the Old Testament when it was used to support the Levitical priesthood.

If we revisit the information about the Pastor from Chapter 5 we can see the biblical roots of the priesthood in the Old testament and the biblical roots of the priesthood in the New Testament:

I.   The Priesthood of the Old Testament
            D. The Patriarchal Period
            E. Israel, a Nation of Priests
            F. The Levitical Priesthood

II. The Priesthood of the New Testament
            G. The Priesthood of Christ
            H. The Common Priesthood of the Faithful
            I.   The Ministerial Priesthood

Our tithes today support the men who dedicate themselves to the work that Christ set before us, much like the tithes of the faithful long ago supported the men of The Levitical Priesthood.

Here are some examples of Early Christians tithing before the time of Cyprian of Carthage:

- Luke 12:33 - Sell your belongings and give alms. Provide money bags for yourselves that do not wear out, an inexhaustible treasure in heaven that no thief can reach nor moth destroy.

- Matthew 6:2-4 - When you give alms, do not blow a trumpet before you, as the hypocrites do in the synagogues and in the streets to win the praise of others. Amen, I say to you, they have received their reward. But when you give alms, do not let your left hand know what your right is doing, so that your almsgiving may be secret. And your Father who sees in secret will repay you.

- From the First Apology of St. Justin Martyr, c. 155 AD:

> *"No one may share the Eucharist with us unless he believes that what we teach is true, unless he is washed in the regenerating waters of baptism for the remission of his sins, and unless he lives in accordance with the principles given us by Christ.*
>
> *We do not consume the eucharistic bread and wine as if it were ordinary*

food and drink, for we have been taught that as Jesus Christ our Savior became a man of flesh and blood by the power of the Word of God, so also the food that our flesh and blood assimilates for its nourishment becomes the flesh and blood of the incarnate Jesus by the power of his own words contained in the prayer of thanksgiving.

*The apostles, in their recollections, which are called gospels, handed down to us what Jesus commanded them to do. They tell us that he took bread, gave thanks and said: Do this in memory of me. This is my body. In the same way he took the cup, he gave thanks and said: This is my blood. The Lord gave this command to them alone. Ever since then we have constantly reminded one another of these things. **The rich among us help the poor and we are always united**. For all that we receive we praise the Creator of the universe through his Son Jesus Christ and through the Holy Spirit.*

On Sunday we have a common assembly of all our members,

whether they live in the city or the outlying districts. The recollections of the apostles or the writings of the prophets are read, as long as there is time. When the reader has finished, the president of the assembly speaks to us; he urges everyone to imitate the examples of virtue we have heard in the readings. Then we all stand up together and pray.

On the conclusion of our prayer, bread and wine and water are brought forward. The president offers prayers and gives thanks to the best of his ability, and the people give assent by saying, "Amen". The eucharist is distributed, everyone present communicates, and the deacons take it to those who are absent.

__The wealthy, if they wish, may make a contribution, and they themselves decide the amount. The collection is placed in the custody of the president, who uses it to help the orphans and widows and all who for any reason are in distress, whether__ *because they are sick, in prison, or away from home. In a word, he takes care of all who are in need.*

We hold our common assembly on Sunday because it is the first day of the week, the day on which God put darkness and chaos to flight and created the world, and because on that same day our savior Jesus Christ rose from the dead. For he was crucified on Friday and on Sunday he appeared to his apostles and disciples and taught them the things that we have passed on for your consideration."

Development of Tithing After the Fall of the Roman Empire

In the Roman Empire when bad things happened, you would report it to the government and they would fix the problem. When the Germanic tribes started conquering the Western Roman Empire in the 4th-5th centuries, these tribes had no plans or infrastructure setup to support the people like the Roman government previously had put in place.

In times of need, people suddenly had no government entity to turn to for help. So they turned to another entity for help: **The Church.**

Here is an example of one situation that took place:

A plague hit and people turned to Pope Gregory and their local bishops for help. Pope Gregory was the one providing care for many of the sick people.

With no civil authority available to help, people thought maybe if I get God on my side he can help. So people also started going to monks and hermits for help.

When the church starts to take over the civic duties that were once ascribed to the Roman Empire, a lot of people start giving to the church in the form of gold, money, buildings, and land. [7]

This practice, that was born out of the need to support the people of the broken Roman Empire, was put in place not because a greedy church clergy voted on it to impose rules on churchgoers, but rather, it was a response to the huge void left by the vacant Roman government that the conquering Germanic tribes were not able to fulfill.

The practice of tithing continues today because most governments have not declared Christianity the state religion and therefore are not in the business of paying for church mortgages and the living accommodations of Bishops and Priests.

Tithing continues because the people of the church, like in the times of the New Testament, prefer to support the few laborers who dedicate their lives to the spread of the gospel through the celebration of the sacraments and the liturgy.

[7] Cook, William R. 2009. *The Catholic Church: A History.*

Chapter 9: Baptism and the Lord's Supper

In school, children diligently recited their prayers. Their teacher, Sr. Euphrasia, was pleased because two months earlier they had received their First Holy Communion and took it very seriously.

The children were used to eating rice morning, noon, and evening so little 10 year old Li asked her why Jesus didn't say "Give us this day our daily rice?"

Sister smiled. "Well, bread means Eucharist."

She explained that we need rice for the body, but that in asking for this bread we are asking for Holy Communion, the food for the soul and the Bread of Life.

In May 1953, when Li made her First Communion, she had asked Jesus in her heart: "always give me that daily bread so my soul can live and be healthy!" Since then Li received Holy Communion every day, but she was aware that the Communists would not like this and they could stop the Mass at any time. She asked Jesus to make sure this would never happen.

It did happen however!

She never forgot the day men entered the classroom and screamed at the children demanding that they hand over any holy objects they had. The terrified children gave up their carefully hand-painted pictures of Jesus, Mary, and the Saints. Then in a fit of anger, the Inspector pulled the Crucifix off the wall, threw it down on the ground and trampled on it screaming: "The New China will not tolerate these grotesque superstitions!" Li, who loved her picture of the Good Shepherd, tried to hide it in her blouse. It was a special image given to her for her First Holy Communion. But, a loud slap on her cheek sent her crashing to the floor.

That day, the police made a sweep of the village, forcing the people into the tiny Church. The Inspector ridiculed them saying they were tricked into believing God is present in the tabernacle. They watched with disbelief, when in a thundering voice, he ordered the soldiers to fire at the tabernacle. All together the people began to pray intensely because their Jesus was in the tabernacle.

In front of them, he grabbed the ciborium and threw the Sacred Hosts onto the floor. Stunned, they turned their gaze away from him and the sacrilegious act he had just carried out, trying to hold back their tears. Little Li froze in horror. Her innocent heart bled for the Sacred Hosts strewn over the ground. "Isn't anyone going to help Jesus?" she wondered.   The Captain continued his insults, interrupting them only to let out his horrible laughter.

"Now get out!" the inspector yelled.

"Woe to anyone who returns to this den of superstition! He'll answer to me!" Before they left, the pastor, Fr. Luke was locked in the large coal bunker in the church, where a small opening helped him to see through to the sanctuary where the Hosts lay strewn on the floor.

The church quickly emptied.

When the communists left, they did not see the small girl who remained praying in the Church. It was Li. As well as Li, there were the angels who are always present around Jesus in the Blessed Sacrament to adore Him, and also there was Fr. Luke who saw, through the opening in his bunker, a beautiful, well dressed woman, approach Li, comfort her, and ask if she would like to leave now with her. Li was glad to do so. She broke into tears before they both left.

Earlier, foreseeing the takeover, parishioners had asked Fr. Luke to be careful. There was little the priest could do. However, upset at all that happened, there was still one thing he could do. He sank into prayers of atonement for the sacrileges committed against Jesus and suffered because he was not able to come to Jesus' defense.

He prayed in anguish.

"Stop this sacrilege! Lord Jesus!" The next day he noticed the arrival of the little girl who silently came into the Church. Slowly, she made her way into the sanctuary. Fr. Luke trembled: she could be killed! Unable to communicate with her, he could only watch and beg all the saints in Heaven to protect this child. He observed her as she bowed for a moment and adored in silence, just as she had been taught to do.

Little Li stayed with Jesus in adoration for one whole hour, knowing that she was to prepare her heart before receiving Him. Her hands joined together, she whispered a prayer to her Jesus so mistreated and abandoned. Fr. Luke never took his eyes off the young girl, and continued to observe her as she lowered herself down on her knees, bent over, and with her tongue, took up one of the Hosts. She remained there on her knees, eyes closed and in deep joy. Each second seemed an eternity to Fr. Luke. If only he could speak to her! However, his fear was gone when the young girl, with a gentle spring in her step, left the Church quietly and unnoticed.

Meanwhile, the Communists searched the entire village to rid it of anything holy. This type of purging was going on throughout the "New China."

Villagers stayed quietly and fearful in their bamboo homes, terrified to venture out. Yet, every morning, Li slipped away to find her Living Bread in the church.

Like on the first day, she repeated the same routine of spending one holy hour in adoration of her Friend Jesus. As before, she then took up one Host with her tongue and left quietly. Fr. Luke, concerned for her safety, couldn't understand why she didn't take more than one. He knew how many Hosts had been in the ciborium: there were thirty- two and surely she would be seen if she came in each of those days?

But, Li didn't do that, as Sister had taught the children they could have only one Host per day and they were never to touch it except with the tongue. The little girl knew just how precious the Host was: it was Jesus Himself really and truly present.

Fr. Luke was relieved when the last day came.

At daybreak, Li entered and drew near to the altar. She knelt to pray, close to Jesus in the Sacred Host. Father Luke had to stifle a cry when a soldier suddenly appeared at the church door and aimed his gun at her.

A single shot was heard, followed by laughter. The child immediately collapsed.

Fr. Luke thought she was dead, but no! Grief stricken, he watched her struggle to crawl over to where the Host was, and could hardly believe his eyes when, in obvious pain, she put her tongue over the Sacred Host to receive her Jesus for the last time. She then drew her last breath and died: a true martyr's death.

The soldier released Fr. Luke, and told him he was free to go. Without hesitation, he rushed to the sanctuary to see Li's lifeless body. As he knelt beside her, the soldier approached. Saddened by his act he said: "Sir, if in every town there was such a little girl, no soldier would ever fight for the Communists!"

Fr. Luke gave Li a decent burial. As he left the cemetery, a man approached, invited him into his car, and left him at the border. The priest escaped death and was now free. That is the reason we know the story of this beautiful young Chinese girl martyr today.

It is Finished

In an earlier chapter we discussed an mysterious reference Jesus made multiple times in the Gospel accounts regarding his hour. He made another mysterious comment:

Let this cup pass from me.

When Jesus was at the Last Supper (Luke 22, John 13, Mark 14), he was taking part in a ritual feast called the Passover Seder. The Seder Meal consists of 4 parts:

- Part 1: a solemn blessing (Kiddush) over the first cup of wine followed by a dish of bitter herbs to remind the Jews of the bitterness of Egyptian bondage.
- Part 2: Little halal (Psalm 113) which was sung and then immediately followed by the drinking of the second cup of wine.
- Part 3: meal is served with lamb and unleavened bread. Then the cup of blessing was drunk.
- Part 4: singing of the great halal (psalm 114-118) and the drinking of the fourth cup of wine, the cup of consummation.

There is an obligation to drink four cups of wine during the Seder. If you did not drink all 4 cups, you did not successfully complete the ritual of the Passover meal.

This seems like a liturgy celebration.

However, Jesus says something odd before skipping the final cup of the Seder meal:

- Amen, I say to you, I shall not drink again the fruit of the vine until the day when I drink it new in the kingdom of God." -Mark 14:25

In Mark 14:26, the apostles sang a hymn with Jesus and went out to the mount of Olives. When Jesus skips the fourth cup, it's the equivalent of a Catholic priest skipping communion in mass.

The fundamental part of the liturgy was overlooked.

When he is in the Garden of Gethsemane he makes this statement:

- He advanced a little and fell prostrate in prayer, saying, "My Father, if it is possible, let this cup pass from me; yet, not as I will, but as you will." Matthew 26:39
- He continued talking about the cup in Matthew 26:42- Withdrawing a second time, he prayed again, "My Father, if it is not possible that this cup pass without my drinking it, your will be done!"

What cup was Jesus talking about? Is he referencing the 4th cup he skipped at the Seder meal?

Jesus said he would not drink of the fruit of the vine until he was in his new kingdom:

- Luke 22:18 - for I tell you [that] from this time on I shall not drink of the fruit of the vine until the kingdom of God comes."
- Matthew 26:29 - I tell you, from now on I shall not drink this fruit of the vine until the day when I drink it with you new in the kingdom of my Father."
- Mark 14:25 - Amen, I say to you, I shall not drink again the fruit of the vine until the day when I drink it new in the kingdom of God."

He was even offered wine drugged with Myrrh in Mark 15:23 and Matthew 27:34 but refused to take it.

However, he did drink wine one more time before he died.

What are we to make of this riddle?
How can Jesus vow to not drink wine again at the last supper, refuse it on the way to the cross, then turn around and ask for a drink right before he dies?

Right before he dies, Jesus says "I Thirst" (John 19:28). They give him a drink and then he says "It is Finished" in John 19:30.

What was finished?

When Jesus said "It is Finished" he was not referring to the work of redemption (we weren't redeemed until Jesus rose again as Paul points out in Romans 4:25).

He was referring to the Final Cup of the Seder Meal. He was referring to the only time he ever mentioned the word Covenant. To Renew a Covenant, we share a meal and that meal is the Eucharist: Jesus body and blood.

Exodus 12 - Describes how the Jews were to avoid the final plague sent to pharoah for not releasing the Jews. You had to eat the lamb and drink the cup, if you didn't, the passover was not complete.

You had to eat the Lamb and Drink the cup to seal the Covenant. And when is the only time in the bible that Jesus mentions the new Covenant? At the last supper (Luke 22:20, Mark 14:24, Matthew 26:28).

To make a further point, the first thing Jesus does after his resurrection is walk with two people on the road to Amayus. They invited him to stay with them and they still did not know he was the resurrected Jesus. In fact, they did not recognize him until the breaking of the bread (Luke 24:30-31). [8]

---

[8] Hahn, Scott. 2018. *The Fourth Cup: Unveiling the Mystery of the Last Supper and the Cross*. N.p.: Crown Publishing Group.

The new Covenant is renewed in the breaking of the bread and the drinking of the cup. We must eat the flesh of the lamb and drink his blood to renew the covenant.

Will this language scare you away as it did to many of Jesus followers in John 6:66 or will you renew the covenant that Jesus died to offer to you.

Chapter 10: Christian Education

Frank and George make a compelling argument in Pagan Christianity for the Pagan roots of Christian education.

They state that since the **use of reason** is derived from Aristotelian logic and that Peter Abalard set up the foundation for the theology of Thomas Aquinas (one of the most influential Catholic Theologians). Faith and reason is the adoption of Pagan Philosophies from Aristotle.

The authors go on to claim that the first followers were apprentices and no school system was ever used.

However, is the use of Christian education truly Pagan or does it have any biblical roots?

Biblical Roots of the Seminary

A biblical justification for seminary education might be made from a number of passages, from Matthew 28:19 (and its emphasis on teaching disciples) to 2 Timothy 2:2 (and its emphasis on leadership training) to Titus 1:9 (and its emphasis on elders being equipped to articulate and defend the faith).

But there is a short passage in Acts that provides a biblical precedent for seminary education in a particularly insightful way.

These verses, which at first glance may not seem overly significant, show the apostle Paul starting a theological training school in the city of Ephesus. As one commentator explains: "In Ephesus, Paul opened a school of theology to train future leaders for the developing church in the province of Asia" (Simon J. Kistemaker, Acts, NTC, 684).

It's unlikely that Paul called it Ephesus Theological Seminary, but in essence, **that is exactly what it was.**

The setting was Paul's third missionary journey (A.D. 52/53–56). After leaving Antioch and traveling through the churches of southern Galatia, Paul made his way to the city of Ephesus. There he encountered a dozen or so disciples of John the Baptist and introduced them to the Lord Jesus Christ, the one to whom John pointed (Acts 19:1–7). Picking up the narrative at that point, Luke writes:

> And he entered the synagogue and continued speaking out boldly for three months, **reasoning and persuading** them about the kingdom of God. But when some were becoming hardened and disobedient, speaking evil of *the Way* before the people, he withdrew from them and took away the disciples, **reasoning daily in the school of Tyrannus**. This took place for two years, so that all who lived in Asia heard the word of the Lord, both Jews and Greeks. - Acts 19:8–10

As Luke explains in verses 9–10, Paul met with a group of believers in a school every day for two years, **reasoning with them about theology**. That, in its essence, is the basic paradigm of seminary education.

From this short passage, three features of the first seminary might be derived. And while we must be careful to avoid twisting a narrative text from Acts into a normative prescription for the contemporary church, these features nonetheless provide helpful parallels for those engaged in seminary education today (whether as students or as teachers).[9]

---

[9] Busenitz, Nathan. 2015. "The First Seminary." The First Seminary. https://blog.tms.edu/the-first-seminary.

Catechetical School of Alexandria

The Catechetical School of Alexandria was set up by John Mark and lasted for almost 4 centuries before it was closed.

This school passed on the Christian faith by training priests and training Christian theologians.

One notable theologian who came out of this school was Ireneaus, who was taught by Polycarp, who was taught by John the Apostle.

In Irenaeus we find a highly developed and systematic theology within 2 generations of the Apostles. Christians have been stubbornly thinking about the faith from the beginning.

During the life of Irenaeus we find him using this theology to battle the heresy of Gnosticism.

The theology of Irenaeus is almost entirely biblical. His insights are still valid today. He did not draw from any philosophers. [10]

---

[10] Barron, Bishop. 2020. *More Church Fathers You Should Know (Part 2 of 3)*. https://www.facebook.com/BishopRobertBarron/videos/435682887316585.

Chapter 11: Reapproaching the New Testament

In Chapter 11 of the book *Pagan Christianity*, Frank and George tell us all the reasons why the church got it wrong:

- The Church and the religious people have misinterpreted the word *Ecclesia*.
- The books of the New Testament are in the wrong order.
- People don't understand the bible and should follow a reputable house church for 10 years or more before they take on the task of starting their own house church.
- etc....

This conviction reminds me of a prominent early Christian: Paul.

Paul was also convinced that the religious people of this new movement had gotten it wrong. So much so, that he was persecuting and brutally murdering those people.

He was convicted.

Then something dramatic happened:

- Acts 9:4 - Saul, Saul, why are you persecuting me?

Even the most well intentioned followers of God get it **VERY** wrong sometimes. Paul was one example of a Jew that got blinded by a hardened heart. He was convinced he was right. But God had to physically blind him first before he would open his heart and mind to possible alternatives.

As you ponder what was read in this book, I encourage you to go back to John 6:66 and meditate on how even the followers of Jesus could become separated from him based on a teaching they didn't agree with.

What teaching is bothering you?

Ask God to open your heart and mind to help you understand the issues that are holding you back from receiving the fullness of his gifts in the Institutional Church.

Chapter 12: A Second Glance at the Savior

The authors of Pagan Christianity state that **Jesus came as a revolutionary**.

This is true.

However, what is the revolution?

What would a revolution look like? Maybe like this:

> People meeting in secret to celebrate the Lords Supper (Eucharist) and being brutally murdered as punishment for this risk.

Despite all of these brutal murders, early Christians continue meeting and the church grows. More and more people are murdered for nearly 300 years before it comes to an end.

And when the persecutions finally come to an end it's the persecutors who are the ones that are converted. The church comes out of hiding and its leaders immediately convene at the Council of Nicea.

That sounds revolutionary.

A church that takes care of the whole community when the Roman government falls?

A church that promotes the dignity of all people and considers men and women equal despite the view of the culture.

A church that accepts, baptizes, and ministers to all regardless of race or religion?

A church that is founded on the apostles and not only survives, but grows to every country and laungugage of the world despite all of the corruption and sin of its members.

That sounds like a revolution.

COVENANTS

The bible is full of Covenants. These covenants are passed down from generation to generation and upheld in the religious context of the institutional church.

Something Jesus did NOT speak out against.

We find Jesus condemning the religious practices and the hypocrites of the Church but nowhere does Jesus condemn the Church as an Institution. You can scour your bible from front to back and you will never find a passage where Jesus condemns the Old Institutional Church of his day.

In fact, not only did he refuse to condemn the Institutional Church of his day, he was a devout follower of the Institutional Church. His parents followed the tradition of circumcising Jesus on the 8th day in Luke 2:21.

Jesus did not condemn the use of Covenants in the Old Institutional Church which ran very deep from Adam to Noah to Moses and to David. In fact, rather than condemning this deeply ingrained church tradition, he adds to it by creating a New Covenant, Luke 22.

That sounds Revolutionary.

It's the only time he mentions covenant, and it's not to condemn this Institutional Church tradition, but to continue it.

Jesus does not shatter the Old covenant, he renews it. His last words: **IT IS FINISHED** (referring to the New Covenant).

The last thing Jesus did with his 12 apostles is celebrate the Passover meal, a church Tradition (read John 6) that has continued since that last supper in every nation, in every language, at every hour, and by all people of the world.

It was Jesus' dying wish that his church and its New Traditions continue beyond the apostles. He recruited 12 to carry on this mission. Those 12 appointed others to carry on the mission.

Will you accept this Church Tradition and the man who instigated this tradition?

Jesus tells us this in Mark 2:22: Likewise, no one pours new wine into old wineskins. Otherwise, the wine will burst the skins, and both the wine and the skins are ruined. Rather, new wine is poured into fresh wineskins."

Jesus got rid of Old Testament Church Traditions to make way for the new Church Traditions:

- Baptism instead of Circumcision
- the Eucharist (Lords Supper) instead of the Passover Meal
- Confession instead of burnt sin offerings
- and to allow the whole world to enter into this New Covenant, not just a chosen people.

The new Church does not abolish the old, it fulfills the old and it's the reason that this organization of broken people, guided by the Holy Spirit, has made it through 2000 years of great times and dark times.

Frank and George are well intentioned Christians and I hope and pray this book will soften their hearts and your heart to the truths that have been in front of us since the time of Christ.

May God Bless You in the name of the Father and the Son and the Holy Spirit. Amen.

Made in the USA
Monee, IL
24 May 2023

34469561R00046